Hands like Eyes

Poems, Songs and Fantasies

Burns Taylor

El Paso, Texas
Maiden Voyage Publishing

Copyright © 2013 Burns Taylor
All rights reserved.

ISBN: 0615839037
ISBN-13: 9780615839035
Library of Congress Control Number: 2013943804
Maiden Voyage Publishing,
El Paso, TX

Photography by Ho Barron
Proofreading by Carolyn Rinehart

With love. To my wife, my sweet Valora,
who listened patiently to these poems with
reverence and gave me her valuable response
with a smile or a shrug.

Acknowledgements

In my development as a poet and writer, my mother was the first teacher who instilled in me a fascination for words. When rain prevented me from attending a friend's birthday party, she said, "Rain, rain, go away; come again some other day."

When I asked her about an unsightly mole on my neck, she said, "A mole on the neck brings money by the peck." And on and on.

My mother had a plethora of rhymes she used to comment on just about everything. Her aphorisms like those tuned my ear to the magic of rhythm and rhyme in everyday speech.

In high school I read Sir Walter Scott and Alfred Tennyson and Ralph Waldo Emerson. At university, though, I was introduced to and immersed in the moderns: Robert Frost, Robinson Jeffers, A. E. Houseman and, of course, Dylan Thomas.

I fell in love with Rupert Brooke's favorite things: "These I have loved: White plates and cups, clean-gleaming, Ringed with blue lines; and feathery, faery dust;" and his cynicism, "all the little emptiness of love."

Later, I came to revere the creative license associated with free verse. I'll never forget one memorable summer afternoon when I was studying in a large room with the windows open. Outside, someone was mowing the lawn. As I picked up Walt Whitman's *Leaves of Grass*, the soporific drone of a gasoline mower and the aroma of fresh cut grass wafted in through the windows as I read, "If you want me again look for me under your boot-soles." I was smitten.

Suddenly I realized that ordinary prose could be elevated for a dramatic effect by using rhythm, varying the length of lines and injecting emotion. After that, I began to see poetry in the prose of Joyce and Faulkner and even Irving Stone.

In graduate school I was mentored by Dr. Robert Burlingame and Joseph Simmons. One day I ran into Joe Simmons going through the magazine rack at the local Safeway market. He had just published a poem in *Harpers Magazine* and was buying up copies. At that moment, success as a writer seemed tangible and near.

But it was as a result of my experience in the MFA program at the University of Southern California that I cut my chops as a professional writer. On a suggestion from one of my writer/teachers, I submitted a piece I had turned in for class credit and hit the jackpot. My three-thousand-word piece was accepted by *Publishers Weekly*. I had made the New York scene. I was ecstatic.

I invited my buddy, Lynn Manning, to join me for drinks and dinner at Barney's Beanery, one of the gathering spots for successful writers in Los Angeles. I was certain I would be immediately recognized as soon as I walked in. I wasn't.

So by reading a lot of dead poets and associating with a lot of live ones, I established my career as a freelance writer.

Contents

Prologue	xv
Alienation and Despair	1
Hands Like Eyes	3
Breakfast Blues	5
Nightscape	6
In the Valley of the Shadow	8
Anonymous Caller	12
Party's Over	14
Voices and Faces	16
At the Diamond Shamrock (For Luke)	18
Dance of the Marionettes	21
After the Reading	23
The Nineties: a View from California	24
Love and Loss	29
The Poem I Might Have Written	30
Surfside	32
Etc.	33
Confession	34
Miraculous Transformation	35
Note Found on a Kitchen Table	36
Let's Pretend (For Gwennie)	38
Before We Say Goodbye: a ballad	39

To Whom It May Concern	41
Pianos	43
Fantasy and Humor	45
Sayonara	46
The Weather Report: a long range forecast	50
Jack Be Nimble	51
Coronation	54
The Wedding	55
Preservation of Pestilence	56
Reflections	57
Street Scene	59
America The Bountiful (with Paul Daniels)	60
Ghetto Christmas (with Glen and Maria Alley)	62
Death and Dying	65
Who Let the Tiger In	66
Dilemma	68
Scars	70
Seasons of my Heart	72
Travelers	75
Yesterdays	76
Sky Words: some lines written above the earth	77
The Way to Armageddon	78
To an Old Guitarist Aging (For Juan Perin)	82
The Bell	84
Ascension	87
New Year's Eve 1994	89
Time and Place	93
Across a Bridge from the Sixties	94
Down at Jonah's	99

El Paso Outback	100
Desert Nocturne	102
La Quinta: Room 227	103
My Sister's Clocks	106
Desert Rain	108
Homecoming	109
The Wall	111
Waiting Room	113
Epiphany	117
Homeless	119
Hymn to Spring	121
Coming Into Autumn	122
Ireland	125
A Farewell to El Paso	126
Autobio	131
Bibliography	135
Index of Poems	139

Prologue

Surely one of the most crucial issues confronting man in the twenty-first century is how to manage the relationship between human beings and technology. The cave man's dependence upon weapons and tools for survival has given way to modern man's use of the computer and the hydrogen bomb to shape his destiny. In a sense, from arming ourselves against a hostile environment in the beginning, we are now at the point of bearing arms against ourselves. The human spirit stands threatened on all sides by the products of man's own genius. But to endure as a species, we must learn to venerate our potential to create more than our power to destroy.

At this point in history, and especially in the United States of America, too many complicated mechanical systems, offensive to human dignity, have been set in motion in the name of "efficiency." We have become a nation of counters and scorekeepers –processed and programmed – gathering statistics and data preciously like manna in the wilderness.

We allow machines to dictate human standards, so that only the neat and the predictable are normal. Less and less tolerance is left for exceptions. We take more pride in what we are able to do than in what we are able to become.

Time and time again the complaint is made that the system will not allow any deviation from the standard procedure. A computer program often determines what can or cannot be done in a given situation. We have become increasingly dependent upon technology – some new software, a new device, upgrades, updates – for answers to our problems.

But remedies for chronic human conditions such as war and poverty will never be found in the computer lab or on the testing range. The solutions to those issues lie within the human heart itself and its capacity for love, compassion and mutual respect.

The evolution of human consciousness to a higher level will not be predicated upon technological advances. The path to spiritual enlightenment is a journey within. The baubles and gadgetry of technology are but an intriguing distraction along the way.

My own journey toward a spiritual awakening is chronicled in these poems written between 1967 and the present. They reflect the perspective of one often marginalized by society because of a disability.

Much of the vocabulary in these poems is taken from business, science and industry because that is the dialect of my time. My choice of imagery and metaphor is often influenced by the senses other than sight because that is the nature of my blindness.

The rhythm of many of my lines comes directly from my experience as a jazz musician. The inflections arise from the cadences of natural speech, since I verbalize all lines before they are written.

A poem, in my view, expresses a way of feeling about a person, a place or an idea. My intention as a poet is to elicit a response from my audience: emotionally or intellectually or both. As a poet, I take a concept, shrink it down to its fundamental density, then inject it with distilled emotion. A poem often seeps into my consciousness like a half-remembered dream that I, like a witness under oath, must strive to recall with all the perspicuity at my command.

Alienation and Despair

LIFE WITH A DISABILITY IS OFTEN LIKE BEING THE ONLY SPECTATOR AT A GAME EVERYONE ELSE IS PLAYING.

Hands Like Eyes

At the school for the blind,
it was the feeling hands, the most.
Like thick legged spiders,
they crawled into all the secret places,
forcing intimacy upon strangers.
They rubbed the wooden banisters silky
and wore down the iron benches.

Hands like creatures with a life of their own:
Long hands with fingers the size of dill pickles;
Short wide hands with stubby fingers
like Vienna sausages;
Tiny withered hands with long thin fingers like pencils.
Hands with a touch as gentle as butterfly kisses.
Blind, inquisitive, intrusive Hands,
like those of a surgeon probing for a tumor.

Hands like eyes,
that rummage through the world around them
like a dog searching for a buried bone,
stretching across the boundaries of
isolation and unknowing,
striving to connect the world of
darkness to the world of light:
grasping at art, caressing faces.

King Touch, overriding all the other channels.
"Blind loving wrestling touch, sheath'd
hooded sharp-tooth'd touch!"
Between reach and contact,
between touch and recognition,
lies the mystery of intention.

Rambunctious, energetic hands,
knocking things over, picking things up:
reading Braille, feeling of signs;
struggling to synthesize a meaningful whole
from the sum of the parts.

Hands like eyes,
touching, squeezing, holding on, wanting to know.
Where am I?
Who are you?
What are we doing here?
What is this made of?
How does it work?
Why is it shaped like this?

Published in Ojo Del Lago ajijic, Jalisco, Mexico-2011

Breakfast Blues

I sit in darkness
in a cold, quiet room,
fantasizing company.

Hello, loneliness,
my old friend;
sit right down.
We're having the blues for breakfast.

Because weekends no longer matter.
That thrill of excitement on Friday night
when you just got paid,
and the scent of night-flowering jasmine
ignites a glandular fever.
But we're having the blues for breakfast.

I fathom the echoes in these empty rooms:
Parceling out ample silences
like coupons clipped from the Sunday paper.

And I hear myself say,
"Hello blues,
Hello breakfast,
May I join you?"

Nightscape

The night is screaming;
then shots ring out
and sirens fill the air.
Somewhere close by,
the sound of running feet.

I close the balcony door,
turn up the music
and light up.

Sometimes when the lights go dim in the evening
and shadows fall,
within those pockets of silence between echoes,
I hear infinities unfolding.

Following the ironclad laws,
making the same old promises,
that tomorrow will be better than today;
that the huddled masses nestled in darkness
behind the fallen curtain will learn patience.

But it is those whispers at night,
those tongue-tied incoherencies
that float over garden walls
at the hush of evening,
that are the most troubling.

Those Spartan compromises,
forged in the fire of threat and violence,
those lies we learn to live with,
solemn covenants never meant to be kept,
that keep us going,
that sustain the illusion of a future.

Published in BORDER VOICES, El Paso, 1994

Winner in the national poetry competition sponsored by the National Federation for the Blind, 2009

In the Valley of the Shadow

I walk in darkness.
Light is only heat:
the sudden warmth of sunshine on my arm, my shoulder.
Light is a fantastic abstraction,
a brash intrusion
that violates the privacy of darkness.

Light is brutal.
It strips a thing of all pretenses,
burns away shadows like fumes,
revealing the cold, glittering truth reflected in surfaces.

Sight is superficial.
It measures appearances only:
reflections, illusions, mirages.
It lacks the intimacy of touch,
the immediacy of smell,
the physical power of sound.

I am blind.
I can open my eyes or close them
and it doesn't make a difference.
Voices, smells and footsteps:
that's all there is of people.

Laughing voices with the metallic ring of a silver dollar
spinning down on a tile bar top;
dainty footsteps down the hall
that enslave the heart to a phantom love,
unseen, never spoken to.
The intoxicating scent of Arpege on an April evening
sends my cravings dancing.

Voices filled with the hard driving
edge of command in them.
Mendicant voices that reach out in filaments,
that plead, then bargain then wheedle,
then snare me in a web.
Liars' Voices.
Lover's Voices:
those breathy ellipses
those gargantuan vacancies
that dwell between naked spirits.

I'm blind.
I cross streets with my eyes closed.
I can tell whether a woman is blonde or brunette
with a fleeting stroke of her hair.

My eyes are silent.
But I read paper money with my fingertips,
measure distances in footsteps,

hear textures,
listen through walls,
smell through glass.

I'm visually impaired.
I speak softly and carry a long, white stick.
I love the musty smell of beer halls,
the clack of pool balls,
the earnest ring of an old-fashioned cash register:
The sexuality of silk and satin,
the warmth of velvet,
the smooth, cool solidity of stone benches in
government buildings.

I'm super blink!
I'm Helen Keller,
Homer, Milton
Stevie Wonder, Ray Charles
Louis Braille, Al Hibbler, George Shearing
all rolled up into one.

And I am the disheveled blind beggar, too,
slumped against the broken stones of the village well
at a desert crossroads
crying out to a passing caravan:
"Alms for the blind!
Alms!
Alms for the blind!"

My eyes are broken,
yet when I inhale, I catch the scent of spring roses
buried in the stench of the rubbish heap;
I touch,
and my fingers find a reality that eludes
the modality of the visible;
I listen,
and I hear shadows dancing in the wind.

Anonymous Caller

"Hello,"   I pray,
I wail.   into the square, flat mouthpiece,

there's nothing.   I hear a faint metallic ringing

an empty line.   Am I on hold?
Is this a scam?   Do we have a bad connection?

"Hello!"   I cry
And the ringing modulates,   And a Mixolydian cluster,
A pentatonic chorus   sings through the line
in a blur of white noise,   like angels' breath.
The cosmic respiration.   And I inhale.

"Hello." I whisper softly   into cosmic waves,
into the web of stellar synapses   riding in on moon beams.
"Are You there? Is anybody there?   Does it really matter?"

This is ridiculous.   Why am I standing here?
No one's listening.   No one's there.
I'm speaking to a ghost.   Who? Is? This?

                    "Hello!"   "Hello!"

"Hello!"   "Hello!"
Shit!   Bang!
AMEN

Party's Over

After the laughter,
when the lights go dim
and pretense vanishes:
The jokes and blandishments swept out with the garbage.
The shared secrets, the bargains,
the plans to reconvene later on.

After the laughter,
when shadows fill the yard
and the cabinets are empty;
your stash is dry
and you gotta husky jones comin' down.

After the laughter,
when the doors click shut behind the last guests,
you turn to the mirror
and try to separate the truth from the lies you've been told.

After the laughter,
alone again:
the dirty dishes, the leftovers,
half empty beer cans filled with cigarette butts.

The residue of revelry hangs in the air
like dank cigarette smoke;

while in a dark corner
crouching like a vulture,
despair licks its chops.

Voices and Faces

Beyond the words, behind the eyes,
bearing secrets like masked strangers.
Faces that conceal the mysteries of the heart;
voices that reveal the temperament of the soul.

Voices like faces,
projecting identities,
flaunting the signatures of egos
like cattle brands.
The emblems of self,
impinging, demanding recognition.

The remembrance of voices grown faint with the passage
of time,
nibbling at the edges of my memory,
vaguely reminiscent like pieces of faces:
habits of speech like noses;
accents like eyes;
timbre like chins.
Voices that hang in the air like smoke
long after the words have vanished.

Fragments of faces
that linger in memory,
like lost puzzle pieces.

Words that melt into images;
Sounds that conjure up visions.

Voices that emerge from a chorus of memories.
Voices in search of a name,
like scraps of familiar tunes I can no longer name.

Faces gone dim like faded photographs.
Jumbled voices that mingle in memory,
then separate, then merge again.
Nameless faces in a lineup;
anonymous voices in a crowd.

Voices like faces,
music like flowers.
Faces of the vanished, voices of the dead.
Faceless voices, floating through time.
The jagged dissonance of phantom and reality
Then a synthesis of melody and harmony
that grips my consciousness with a startling presence,
that haunts my dreams;
so familiar it makes me call out in the night,
"Is that you, Tom?"

At the Diamond Shamrock
(For Luke)

Day after day, I've watched you,
leaning all spraddle-legged up against the back of the building:
grease-stained shirt, bronzed knees showing through tattered jeans.

Now you walk up to me;
your breath tinged with the scent of stale wine.

"Any spare change, mister?" you ask.
You say it so glibly now,
not like the first time
when it must have hung in your throat like a fish bone;
when you vomited up the last morsel of your pride
into the cracked, oil streaked, sun bleached pavement
behind the Diamond Shamrock,
then slept in the vomit.

Charlie I've got thousands in tax sheltered annuities.
I'm vested in my company so I will retire at 3 quarters pay
for the rest of my life.
I own ten thousand shares of blue chip stock
and part interest in a South African diamond mine.
I'm black. I have apartments,
I have a portfolio full of municipal bonds.

And you stand before me here
so young, so strong–asking me for change.
You're white, Charlie, and free.
You were born with all the privileges
and few responsibilities.
I can see it in your eyes,
that pampered look white boys have
when they have to ask their mamas.

You never had to sit at the back of the bus.
You never suffered that cramp that strikes like a thunderbolt in the pit of your stomach
when they turn you away
because of the color of your skin and for no other reason.

When I was your age, Charlie, I joined the Army.
Couldn't find no legitimate job.
Served in the Pacific, War Two. Guadalcanal.
Traded in a shattered knee and two fingers on
my right hand
for a purple heart.

When I came out of the Army,
I got a job hauling gravel for 25 bucks a load.
Then I roofed for a while before I went into civil service.
When I noticed that only the white folks around me got promoted, though, I quit.

Then I developed a self-shining black boot gloss
for the Army,
and that really made it for me.

So that's it, Charlie! There's your answer.
Join the Army, man, get yoself some pride.
But no!
You rather stan' out heah and hit on
folks for spare change.

Shit, man! Check me out!
This shark skin suit and these radical Stacey Adams kicks?
I ain' ee'n gon' mention the gold.
You think they came easy?

Nah, man. Screw you, Charlie.
I ain' got no change fuh yo funky white ass today, Chump.
You see, I gotta cash flow problem, Charlie.
Like the smallest unit of expendable capital
I happen to have on my person at the moment
is a C note, Jack.
You dig?

Dance of the Marionettes

Who pulls the strings
we do not know,
we're simply here
to put on a show.

What's our next move
we cannot say,
the strings grow taut
and we obey.

No need to think,
we do as we're told;
if we move out of sync,
the show may fold.

What hand us moves,
we cannot see,
we dance and sing
and pretend we're free.

We wear the right costumes
the hat and the gloves,
then wait for directions
which come from above.

We're told what to think,
when to breathe, what to wear,
but we never object,
how could we dare?

The roles we play
come down from on high,
one day we laugh,
the next day we cry.

We bow to the master,
we creep and we kneel,
just bumps on a log,
cogs in a wheel.

After the Reading

They saw the handwriting on the wall,
and finding it was in Braille,
summoned the government magicians.

Tongues waggled,
brains wrangled,
while the strangled town
slept long into the oiled road summer,
fearing insects.

But the wisemen's elders,
swaggering in the heat,
fathomed the sign of the oracle
splashed in the cracked stones:
the stammering prophecy
chiseled in the broken wall.

And the scholars and the monks,
clumping through the long-town, summertime heat,
heads bowed,
speaking in tongues,
knew they were past saving.

The Nineties:
a view from California

It's lonesome out here in the Nineties,
so far from home.
No room left for my love beads and sandals;
they're up in the attic with my peace symbol and the
dashiki, too.

But how did they manage to turn it all around so fast?
Wasn't there a revolution on the agenda?
Didn't the soul brothers say,
"When the revolution come,
you'd better buy yo honkie ass a ticket to Scandinavia?"

But it never happened.
The music's all different now,
and drugs got a bad reputation.
That wasn't in the plan.

We were going to toke our way into that interracial,
intergalactic, Woodstockian brotherhood of love
that we paid down on
with Kennedy and King and Kennedy
and Jimi and Janice Joplin, too.

That readiness to love, that infatuation with change,
that belief that everything could eventually be cured

was intended to carry us through to nirvana or
the crystal palace
or whatever.

But now there's rehab and 9 1 1 and AIDS
and the price of an ounce of weed in California
is about the same as an ounce of gold in New York.

It's boring out here in the Nineties.
We caress our electronic cocks,
touting their features brashly,
mesmerized by their power, their satisfaction,
their guarantee.

Love is metered now, like a taxi ride.
We sit here, counting the clicks in our ears,
uncertain if we'll be able to pay the fare
when we reach our destination.

It's cold out here in the Nineties.
We can no longer hope to be forgiven
for what we don't remember.
The pizza we ordered last night is still in the computer.
They know where we sleep, what we eat, who our
friends are.

It's not like the old days,
when papers could get lost and calls could still be
made anonymously.

We were less accountable then:
Freer to improvise,
in love with possibilities.

But now I'm told when to water my grass,
warned not to burn wood in my fireplace on certain days.
For this, they slaughtered our youth at Corregidor?
For this we mortgaged our souls in Vietnam?

It's scary out here in the Nineties:
living on the edge of the "big one,"
updating my insurances.

Somehow I know that love will never come to me again
like a surprise between strangers.
One must be tested for that now,
have the proper credentials.

Relationships are not "screwed up,"
they're defective.
And these soft-bellied, candy-assed milkmen out here
would never even dream of spawning bastards.

They only make love under contract;
grew up with condoms in their Crackerjacks;
open doors with paper towels,
shake hands with their gloves on.

We are aliens out here in the Nineties–afraid to stray from the beaten path,
too vulnerable ourselves to ask questions.
So I kneel and pray to Alf in a whisper,
spring sunshine bleeding through the Venetian blinds
"halaluhya waaya!
"halaluhya waaya!
Welcome to the Nineties.

Love and Loss

YOU NEVER KNOW HOW MUCH YOU REALLY LOVE SOMETHING OR SOME ONE UNTIL YOU COME TO LOSE THEM.

The Poem I Might Have Written

You could have been the subject of
the poem I might have written;
I would have praised your beauty and
proclaimed that I was smitten.
I could have extolled in great detail
your curves and hair and sexy smile.
But the words somehow eluded me
eschewed my wit and guile.

The poem I might have written,
like the song I might have sung,
beneath the moon that could have risen,
like the bell that went unrung.

If we never speak those feelings that make us want to sing,
we may never know the happiness that honesty can bring.
If we conceal the real emotion that lies within our hearts,
we may spend our lives in loneliness and always live apart.

Don't let the music die within,
like the song you've never sung,
and the words you've never spoken
like the deed that goes undone.

Would I could have found a song
of love to send to you my kitten,
but my muse refused to collaborate,
so the page lies blank on my desk in wait,
your grace and charms to celebrate
in the poem I might have written.

Surfside

Wind-blown,
sky-domed,
the rising tide foaming at our feet;
driven by the same old animal lust,
where, the only answer.

Moments later,
the two of us,
love racked,
huddled flat against the packed sand;
our bodies one,
crotch-hinged,
flesh arched by the pounding pulse,
taken from the sea's incessancy.

Etc.

Strange hotels in foreign cities:
sleeping long into the day that lavender summer;
practicing love without a license,
on a travelers' check holiday at the fairgrounds.
Like two teenagers throwing tennis balls for Kewpie Dolls.

Lazy afternoons in the barroom,
listening to one who used to be someone else
speak of his collection of rare bottles and old tiles.
Wrote novels under a pseudonym he could no longer remember.

Made of glass, dying on camera,
sharing his past with us shyly
like a peek into a chest full of diamonds.

Out on the roof garden with old Dick,
who told us
how he sucked smoked monkeys' brains through their eye sockets,
way up the Amazon,
and so on,
etc.

Confession

Suddenly I want to say I love you.
Not as a confession of the truth,
but to elicit a response from you.

Because it would be unthinkable,
to let this moment pass and say nothing.

So out of fear and loneliness,
to stave off the awful agony of silence,
I say it and I am amazed
by the slow, painful leaking from your eyes.

Love was never meant to hurt like this,
never meant to signal an ending.
Love is the emblem of hope
that binds two lives together.

I feel free enough to take a chance,
to risk my own complicity in a lie.
So I say it again aloud,
"I love you."

Because there is nothing more to say
to fill the emptiness between us.
It dribbles from the corner of my lip
like vagrant wine, and it sounds like "Goodbye."

Miraculous Transformation

We lay in a grassy field,
bathed in April starlight.
Your velvet voice soothed my anxious mind.
And I slept.

I dreamt I sculpted your ample breasts in my hands,
kissed your full lips deeply and caressed your
alabaster skin.
My fingers plied the pliant flesh of your calves and thighs,
as I inhaled the perfume from the silken tresses
of your hair.

We romped through the countryside, exultant,
reinjecting ourselves with the fervor of our youth.
I, the vampire; you, the witch.

But when I awoke,
what I cradled in my arms,
rattling like a handful of wooden spoons,
was your skeleton.

Note Found on a Kitchen Table

3 p.m., Tuesday, leaving.
I'm taking my records
and a pack of Winstons I found in your raincoat.
I'm going to a foreign country
that has no flag, no anthem,
where water is free,
and the king and queen had to get married.

I plan to go into the funnies business
with a couple of comic strip characters I met
down at the newspaper.

If I don't get raped in the park,
mugged at the movies,
or stoned by the rabble,
I'll be back in spring.

Thanks for everything;
it was a hell of a ride.
The wine, the roses.
An empty bottle, a broken glass,
and I'm gone.

Tell Old Sandy
I'll look for him in New Orleans at Mardi Gras time.
And don't forget to take your vitamins.

PS
Key's in the flowerpot; dope's in the Igloo.

Let's Pretend
(For Gwennie)

It's you, before I answer the phone.
I know before I open the door, it's you.
Every ringing phone, every knock at the door,
a disappointment.
It's you, all the time,
until I find out it isn't.

It is the pretense that makes life bearable:
the trick I play on myself
that holds you freeze-framed in the present moment,
that keeps you perpetually locked in my heart.
After every funny story I tell,
I hear your raucous laughter.
After every infuriating incident,
I feel your anger.
There's all the news
I long to share with you,
but can't.

Hey! What do you say?
Let's just pretend that you're still in this world.
Let's make believe we'll meet some day
on a sunny street in Rio
or Paris
or Samarkand.

Before We Say Goodbye: a ballad

Before we say goodbye,
is there anything that I
could say to change your mind?
Before we bid adieu,
is there anything that I
could do to touch your soul?

We stand here on the brink of forever,
the end of our lives together.
But before we drift apart,
listen with your heart,
is there anything I could say to change your mind?

Is this that fond farewell,
where I say I wish you well,
and walk away alone?
Before we say so long,
let's forget who's right or wrong,
and make a brand new start.

We stand here on the brink of forever,
the end of our lives together.
But before we drift apart,
listen with your heart,
is there anything I could say to change your mind?

The times we spent together
still live in my mind:
those golden afternoons in strange hotels.
So before we call it a day
and just throw it all away,
is there anything at all that I could say?

Before we say goodbye,
is there anything that I
could say to change your mind?
Before we bid adieu,
is there anything that I
could do to touch your soul?

We stand here on the brink of forever,
the end of our lives together.
But before we drift apart,
listen with your heart,
is there anything I could say to change your mind?
Anything I could say to change your mind?

To Whom It May Concern

If I were to run into you
after all these years,
at the mall, say, or the supermarket;
I'd probably say something totally goofy like,
"que te pasa, Calabasa?"
And you would most likely reply with,
"nada, nada, Limonada."

After all those long rides
through valleys of promise
waiting for some magic to happen.
with Butch Cassidy and the Sundance Kid
Trio Los Ponchos,
and those hot afternoons of passionate lovemaking
that left paradise on hold.

But the magic never happened.
So when you found out the house I appeared to own was
merely rented,
it was over for you.
And the first time you took your shoes off in my house
and I was shocked by the odor,
that's pretty much when I knew it was all over for me.

I'd still like to hear, though:
where you are,

how many kids you've got
and what you've been doing since 1970.

So if you're somewhere out there,
reading this,
you know who you are;
I'm in the phone book.

Pianos

I've known celebrity pianos:
majestic instruments,
pampered with lace coverings and fine tunings,
with skin as hard and smooth as glass.
Commanding the center of attention:
ponderous, deep-throated pianos
that belched bass notes like thunder in your guts.
Concert grands that intimidated,
dared you to measure up to their high standards.

I've played pianos
that stood naked with broken hammers and
twisted strings,
strangling in the heat of a dingy bar:
savaged by drunks,
with some keys that merely clicked when you struck them:
Out-of-tune pianos
that could, on any given night,
gather their meager resources
and sing like a tenor at the Met.

I've jammed on rickety old pianos
with loose action and missing ivories,
that filled me with peace and joy:
and brought me lovers,

and made me friends,
and strove to convince me that I was better than I was.

I've stroked pianos:
slutty pianos that posed like whores
in semi public places,
waiting for their next piano John to come along:
Where practice became performance
as strangers lingered at the door,
hesitated for a moment,
then smiled and moved on.

I've had quiet affairs with lonely pianos
in hidden rooms:
dusty and tuneless,
untouched for years,
aching for a chance to sing.
Pianos I turned to in desperation
that gave me back a song,
that mended my heart.

Fantasy and Humor

FANTASY AND LAUGHTER: THE BEST WAY I KNOW OF TO REBOOT THE BRAIN IN A POSITIVE LIGHT, LEGALLY.

Sayonara

There should be some sort of signal I could give her, some way of telegraphing it.
I don't know. . . I mean we both know it's over between us.
At least I do.
I wanna tell her,
"Look, I'm a lot more comfortable at home when you're not there."
But then part of me wants to say something really cold-blooded and mean, something that would convince her immediately that any fire I ever had for her has turned to ice.
Then I think of doing things to fester antipathy in her, to lower myself in her esteem, to cause her to lose respect for me. Let's face it. If I can cause her to hate me enough to just walk away, then I don't have to do anything, won't have to make a decision.
I could just go on a three-day drunk: come home wearing a new suit with lipstick on the collar of my silk shirt, smoke some herb in the living room, piss in the bathroom sink and leave after making several whispery phone calls. I might even slap her around a little on the way out the door. That would do it.
Yet part of me feels sorry for her. She has no friends. I count up the numbers and wonder how she could possibly make it financially without me. I see her growing

old alone, her life essentially over – fumbling for her key in a darkened hallway that reeks of stale piss and vomit. The sagging floor squeaks before a shaky door.

She dreams sleeplessly of those times when we had a home in the suburbs with wide lawns and a view of the ocean. Now rats devour the studs in the walls, her rent is due and she can't remember if she took her medicine.

Truth is, she'll probably do a lot better on her own without me. Then I try to cancel out my guilt feelings by substituting anger and hate. I focus on the negatives: the time she failed to show up for my big performance; the time she really wasn't there for me when my mama died. And pretty soon I feel like being totally cold and heartless.

I'm going to tell her that I never really loved her, that I married her under pressure from her family and friends. I'll swear that sex was never good with her because she always parceled it out like the mandatory apple in the sack lunch at a church picnic.

Then I remind myself that these lines are rehearsed. I've said all these things a thousand times before. So what does that make me? A fucking wimp?

That's it! In the name of equality of the sexes, I have become enslaved by a crass, not-so-bright government worker. How in the hell did I get tied up with a woman like this in the first place. Now I have a gender complex.

I gaze at the 8 by 10 photo on the wall across from my desk: the one of her surprise bridal shower. She was so slim, so voluptuous, her face so full of promise. But that promise is thirty years gone from her eyes now.

Her eyes glow dully, like two flashlights with dying batteries.

I think of telling her,

"Hey, Bitch! It's just that you are of no further use to me. Get it?" But I know that I could never say anything like that to her. And it pisses me off at the same time because I couldn't.

Why couldn't she just find somebody new. I consider some possible replacements. She's not a bad looking old gal, even now. A little lumpy around the middle, maybe, but still holding her figure at sixty.

Then I catch myself feeling a little jealous of her being with someone else and say,

"Uh uh. Not this time. I done made up my mind, Jack. This movie's over."

And I picture myself in my new apartment. Should I go for a stylish one-bedroom or opt for more room in a cheaper two-bedroom? A classy one-bedroom would be better for entertaining.

Shit! It's going to come down to how much I end up with. She'll probably hook up with one of those young, hungry Yankee lawyers, come South to hone his fangs on easy meat. And I worry if he'll find those hidden annuities, if he'll try to go after my future inheritance.

Goddamn it! The roof's on fire. It's time to start siphoning off the checking and savings accounts before she really knows what's happening. Time to get the jump, old boy, I tell myself.

I'll just be cool and act like there's nothing going on: find an apartment, line up the move and start packing my shit surreptitiously, one box at a time, into storage so she doesn't see anything sitting around.

Then when the day comes for the movers to arrive, I'll step up to her one breezy afternoon in April on the way back to work after lunch, smiling, wearing my stone-washed jeans with a red flannel shirt and say,

"Sayonara, Babe! See you next karma, eh?

But here she is again, coming up behind me and pressing her warm cheek against my bare neck. Fuck it! It's all over again. What little resolve I had drains right down through my shoes. Suddenly, I've got a surprise erection working now. First time in six months. and I realize I could never leave her. We've been through so much together.

Besides, it's Monday evening. My turn to take out the garbage.

The Weather Report: a long range forecast

Dawn will occur as usual in the morning at exactly 6.2 Intergalactic Universal Time. After an illumination threshold of one hundred thousand footcandles has been exceeded, a slight cloud cover will be produced in order to establish a constant sixty percent humidity level throughout this entire cycle. The clouds will be dissolved once that reading has been stabilized.

The high temperature, a very comfortable 75.3 Morzat units, will be attained at precisely 25.5 p.m. IUT.

Here in the Southwest Sector, the overhead chemical precipitation synthesizers will be activated on alternate work days, in order that the internal atmosphere may be scrubbed clean of all defective electrons.

This entire operation will be especially entertaining for you young folks out there and boy! It should be a real dose of nostalgia for those few old-timers who may remember rain.

Finally, for the really good news.

A strike settlement has been hammered out between Meteorological Systems Inc. and Weather Programmers United, so there will definitely be snow for Christmas.

Jack Be Nimble

The embittered knight stood upon the brawling shores
of the light of life,
bristling with Asia.
Convinced that oceans could never be wide enough,
he fastened on the wax wings,
fell and broke his crown.

And then the warden stepped in and told Jack,
"Man, we're puttin' you away for five hundred million
years plus ten."

Jack moved uneasily.
It was a huge room.
The scream of distant sirens filled the air.
Outside, word ran through the streets
that the royal outposts
had just been overrun by the ancient priests of Argenon.
Still they would not cease from marching against the others,
because the Referee said so.

"But that's no reason," said Jack.
"History cannot preside at every inquest.
After all, Jonah didn't swallow the whale, you know.
And besides, I hear that if you can just jerk the

foundations out from under your institutions quickly enough,
they won't even wobble."
"But the Savior is too close at hand for that now," he said,
lying about his dreams.
   "My ancestors discovered fire in the north.
They hoarded the precious flames like water in winter
and camped by the ashes in the heat.
Sleeping in caves,
they watched the vultures die of hunger,
hanging by chains from a broken sky.

Huddled by the sacred fires,
they sang the song of remembering
not to tell the secret they had long ago forgotten."

   "Yep, we're gonna have to take her out all right," said the doctor.
   Jack felt himself grow cold on the stone table. "What's that?" he asked.

"Your memory," said the oracle with snakes in his hands.
"It's the only way we're going to get you back to "now."
We're placing you under arrest
for suspicion of having plagiarized the Bible.
Morals charge!
You are henceforth the property of and for the state of blank from
the date: blank forward.

Your new life begins today.
Whatever you may say or do will no longer be held against you.
But if you cannot jump over this candlestick . . .
We're putting you away for . . ."

"That's enough, your honor," said the vultures with beaks of chain.
And Jack was convicted by the oracle for jumping too high,
sold on the auction block,
then later traded for a color TV and one week's free vacation in the State Asylum for the Blind.

Coronation

Packed in a taxi full of redheaded gypsies
on the way to a coronation;
past dogs dressed like fireplugs
and pieces of broken toilets
transformed into flowerpots.
And that girl... what was her name?
Locked in a cage down by the river.
Only I had forgotten my key.
And I was late for the coronation.
But I asked the taxi driver to stop by anyway,
to see what he could do.
What was her name???
That girl locked in the cage down by the river.
Then I remembered I had swallowed the key.

But when we got to the river,
it was all gone: girl, cage, everything.
And the dogs dressed like fireplugs
danced to the music played by the redheaded gypsies.
And soon the river was gone, too.
So I drove myself to the coronation
in a hijacked taxi.
But it was over by the time I got there.
And when I tried to crash the party,
I was arrested by a fireplug
dressed like a red-haired girl named gypsy.

The Wedding

Cecil and Mildred got married;
    it seemed like a wonderful plan.
The occasion was blessed
    with sumptuous largesse
and the gathering of all the clans.

The pair got along like ding and dong,
    for never did they fight or feud.
But then one day,
    to their great dismay,
Cecil ceased
    and Mildred mildewed.

Preservation of Pestilence

Ladies and gentlemen! Realizing that emergency measures must be taken to protect those vanishing hordes of bacteria, viruses and fungi which have been virtually annihilated by the onslaught of modern science, I am proposing the formation of a brave, new organization: the Society for the Preservation of Pestilence.

Government laboratories and nurseries have been created to foster the growth and development of some of the most virulent bacteria known to man. Did you know, for example, that bubonic plague is now closer to extinction than the buffalo ever was?

Just think of it! Your own grandchildren may never know what it was like to have mumps or measles, to say nothing of whooping cough.

So throw away all of those antibiotics and make your body safe for disease-causing organisms. Take care of the germs you meet today and chances are they'll take care of you.

Join the Society for the Preservation of Pestilence and get sick just as fast as you can.

Reflections

So what's wrong with talking to yourself?
God did it.
Who else was present when He said,
"Let there be light."

Which brings up an interesting question.
When God uttered that command,
was He addressing it to Himself
or was He instructing some other subordinate deity
to do the creating?

If God handled the creation personally,
then it was grammatically incorrect of Him to order Himself to do so by
using the imperative mood of the infinitive (to let),
since the imperative form of the verb always implies either a second
person singular or a second person plural pronoun as the subject:
(You let, you all let).

Therefore, the use of the imperative in God's case suggests the
existence of an orderer and an orderee, or two distinct personalities, or perhaps more appropriately,
two separate entities.

Otherwise, if God were speaking to Himself in Genesis I in either
the second person singular or second person plural,
the only logical conclusion is that Creation, itself, is the product of Divine schizophrenia, or a split in the personality of God.

Thus, substance and form, matter and spirit,
body and soul are all manifestations of a basic division born from a
severe identity crisis
in the mind of God.

Street Scene

Took a ramshackle tram down to Sampan Sam's,
saw an organ grinder jacking off his monkey on the way.
Should have gone to Gorgeous George's Smorgasbord
instead.

America the Bountiful
(with Paul Daniels)

Out of a mass of tangled limbs, a sea of kisses,
out of a lifetime of living out a broken promise–
he went down;
knowing the most he could lose was temporary
desensitization:
a passing that he had experienced to the extent
that he knew when it was happening.

Tubes blowing, sirens going,
and his mind stoking like a Bessemer furnace.

"The lid is definitely going this time," he screamed
into a United States post office mailbox,
as it devoured him with the licentiousness and
shimmering, metallic passion
that a cosmos has for a swaggering nation's
blue-eyed pride.

Why did he not listen to the words of the prophet
raging down at Woolworth's,
his booming voice spewing out of a soda straw?

But it was too late then;
    they were carrying the prophet away from the corner.
Screaming and damning,

he pulled slats of aluminum siding
from the simulated cathedrals of their minds,
splashing images of winos
   emptying their pains of original sin
   into the toilet of vomitless wealth.

Ghetto Christmas
(with Glen and Maria Alley)

                Yo sister lost her job;
yo brother's drinkin' wine.
They done repossessed the slay,
and Santa's doin' time.
So tear up that letter
and make up yo mind,
Santa ain' comin' this year.

                Ghetto Christmas
I ain' got a dime,
wanna buy my kids somethin' new.
All they ever get is broken or used;
just can't shake these Christmas blues.

                Can't afford no turkey
'cause the food stamps are low;
so forget about the tree
and cancel the snow.
I know you want an Xbox and a so-and-so,
but Santa ain't comin' this year.

                Ghetto Christmas
I ain' got a dime;
wanna buy my kids somethin' new.

All they ever get is broken or used;
just can't shake these Christmas blues.

        Toys for Tots say donations are down;
they don't deliver in yo part of town.
So wipe off that smile
and put on a frown
Cause Santa ain' comin' this year.
No, No,
Santa ain't comin' this year.

Death and Dying

"ONE DAY WE ARE BORN; ONE DAY WE WILL DIE; THE SAME DAY; THE SAME INSTANT..." Samuel Beckett

Who Let the Tiger In

This is how it always ends: my nightmare.
A tiger comes padding down the hall.
Trapped in my bedroom,
blind and alone,
I'm armed with nothing but a pillow.

I hear his visceral rumblings at my doorway;
I smell his fetid breath,
as I cringe in impotent rage.
But I always awaken before I'm eaten.

And though I know I'm dreaming this,
there is a tiger out there, somewhere:
prowling through the shadows,
waiting for a chance to come for me, for you.

The tiger haunts my waking hours.
Sometimes when I round a corner
or walk through darkness,
I catch his scent.

Sometimes I hear him move,
rustling the dead leaves,
just there behind the bushes.

Sometimes he appears in a constellation
in a darkening sky.
And I fear falling asleep,
perchance to dream a different ending.

Dilemma

Just there, in the near distance,
drunk with my scent,
their triumphant yelps echo through these woods.

They are close at hand now;
their thick feet rustle the deep leaves beneath the trees.

Down there, below me,
the waters run swift and cold.

Turning back is to surrender all hope.
Ahead sleeps the promise of uncertainty,
but it is the path of my own choosing:
my last act of freedom.
And yet,

the waters run swift and deep down there:
Swift and cold and deep down there.

I hear their labored breathing from the chase.
The gurgling, slobbery growl of conquest in their throats.
My options are gone.

Ever closer to the edge,
I ready myself for the leap into infinity.
And yet,

the waters down there run deep and cold and swift:
Swift and cold and deep down there.

SCARS

Battle scars:
the short thick one just there above my eyebrow.
Stumbled into a cement pillar one evening on my way to class.

"I see bone," the doctor said.
Took six stitches to close that gash.

Those long, thin abdominal scars,
grown faint with time,
hernia surgeries from nearly 50 years ago.

Those unfamiliar scars:
emblems of forgotten injuries,
that make you laugh because of where they are,
and the clearly visible ones you have to explain.

Then there are those deeper scars,
that leave no palpable traces:
The hidden ones that run straight to the heart;
those indelible spiritual scars,
vestiges of the pain that lingers long after the healing.

Those wounds that make your soul bleed a little:
Brands stamped into us by the Beast of Mortality;

event markers that map the trail of a spirit's journey through war zones.

SCARS.

Seasons of My Heart

As a boy,
lying awake in my attic room on North Street,
those quiet summer nights in Austin, Texas,
if I set my head just right with my ear turned into
the pillow,
I heard a faint, rhythmic crunching sound.

I didn't know then what caused it,
but I knew it was me,
my body, doing it somehow.

I imagined a man walking down a friendly road
with a knapsack slung over one shoulder,
his feet softly crunching the leaves.

It was a young man, the footsteps were firm;
the road seemed full of the promise of the morning of
the first day.
And I thought that man could tramp down that
road forever
through an endless autumn morning.

In my prime,
having had my way with some randy college girl,
my ears ringing with the silence of a winter's night,
I heard the footsteps once more.

The autumn afternoon was golden;
half an eternity lay upon the road.
The man, a little older now,
seemed to have a destination in mind.
There was the stress of urgency in his stride:
the intention to get somewhere on time.

But I knew what made the sound of the footsteps by then.
It was the pulse of my carotid artery
thumping against the pillowcase
just enough to crinkle it faintly in my ear.

And I tried to meter those footsteps,
to gauge, somehow, the distance the man had traveled
and how many miles still lay upon the road.
I wanted to fit that number into an equation
that would explain the relationship between time and speed and distance.

Years later,
I know that I and the man are one and the same,
and I listen to those footsteps with an anxious ear;
they sound a little tentative now, the pace has slackened some.

The road seems lonesome.
I feel the chill of the crisp clear evening in my bones.
I know now that the sound of those footsteps
is the sound of death marching through my veins.

At times I hear them even in a crowd.
They click in my head with the monotonous ticking of a metronome.
And remembering the old formula,
I try to calculate the distance I have left to travel.

I wait and listen for the feet to stumble.
Because I know the man will pause by the side of the road one day,
foot suspended above the leaves in mid stride,
bronzed in time.
And today will become forever.

Travelers

The boundaries are blurred;
I feel for the edges.
Where does reality end, where do I begin?

The journey is endless,
and the road is eternal;
where we get on is the same spot where we get off.

Change is the ultimate illusion;
it is how we entertain ourselves between eternities.

Swearing allegiance to heresy,
we hedge our bets in secret,
against the promise of salvation.

Then we stumble on,
like a blind man
clinging to the end of a taut rope,
hoping against hope
to be dragged into Paradise
by whatever's on the other end.

Yesterdays

We are the old ones:
the has-beens, the could have beens, the wannabees.
Worshiping at the shrine of our yesterdays,
when we gloated over our sexual conquests.

Now we compare blood pressures and cholesterol counts,
sharing a wooden park bench
on an overcast summer afternoon.

Planning our retirements,
checking our insurances;
praising the day
when our feet don't touch the floor at six a.m.

We are the old ones:
eyes grown dim, libidos in check,
appetites all diminishing.

Still we find the courage to face another day,
fearful that our bones may shatter should we fall;
prayerful that our feet will lead us home.

Sky Words:
some lines written above the earth

Needles of starlight pierce the earth below me;
distant mountains silhouetted in moonlight.
I measure the distance I have to go
against the time I have to get there.
The quotient is frightening;
my parachute's on fire.

Heaven beckons beneath my feet,
while Hell scorches at my back.
This sail, designed to set me down in green pastures,
now threatens to consume me.
My parachute is burning.

Suspended in space,
between perdition and deliverance,
trailing a tail like a flaming bride's train,
I drift into gravity's embrace.

Will I gently land beside those deep, still waters,
or will I simply perish in the sky?

The Way to Armageddon

This is the land where anything goes:
where fathers sodomize their children,
where our progeny murder each other in the streets
over a bag of drugs.

We have become a predatory race,
preying on our young,
betting that intellect will eventually come to our rescue;
and the gods will return to their senses.

But the air is poison now:
the water, the earth.
And those money whores
pimping their mammon on Wall Street
don't hear the whimpers of the children:
shackled in sweat shops,
afraid to cry out loud.
Is this the way to Armageddon?

It is the hollowness of things,
men most of all,
that echoes through this vacant land.
We are the hollow men:
shadows of our ancestors,
whiskers on the ass of Cro-Magnon.

And I revel in the thought
that fortune could strike on a one-dollar ticket;
I could be a millionaire tomorrow.
But in the darkest corner of my mind
lurks the question that gnaws my conscience like a worm:
Is this the way to Armageddon?

In the evenings,
when the stars are silhouettes through a filmy haze,
I hold my breath sometimes.

When I was young, we fished the lakes
and ate what we caught for dinner.
We drank deeply from the sweet, clear water
and breathed the cool clean air all night.
Awakened from a sound sleep
to the splish-splash of silver bass
breaking water at dawn–knowing that gravity
would prevail
as they leapt into infinity.

But now the lake is a cesspool
and all bets are off.
The air is thick; the sky is low and leaden,
and there's a stranger asking at my door,
"Is this the way to Armageddon?"

It is dangerous to go abroad in these times;
our children are armed against us.

They walk the streets high on drugs,
carrying automatic weapons.
The government, sworn to protect us,
is slowly going bankrupt.

We live behind steel bars,
envied by those who would hijack our cars.
Only the guilty are truly free;
ain't much left for you and me.
Someone tell me could this be:
the way to Armageddon?

But that's just bunk someone jeers;
they've been claiming that for years.
"The children today have gone to the dogs,"
they quote the Greeks from 400 B.C.

But the Greeks are gone now;
their future is in heaven.
And the children of Athens
didn't tote AK47's.

Somewhere a child is crying,
but the blood runs cold in our veins.
Our nerves of steel are deadened.
Somewhere a child is dying
and we really don't give a damn.
So this is not a rehearsal; it's a take.
And we are definitely,

beyond a shadow of a doubt,
on our way to Armageddon.

To an Old Guitarist Aging
(For Juan Perin)

How many miles have your hollow hands fled
down the rough dead vines of your singing tomb?
Like two old hounds, deep in the woods,
baying an apology for the lost scent;
like crippled doves with wilting wings,
they search the strings for a song long since forgotten.

Fondling the guitar in your lap, shyly,
like a wounded bird;
flaunting your shrouded love for a dead self's soul,
sans shame, sans hate.

Play on!
Play on till the walls cave in,
and the din of applause for your dirge
surges like the last sea against the burning crags.

Play on!
Till blind men see
and the deaf can heft your tunes
with their hungry ears.

Cradle your coffin close
in the driest year of a shriveling century.
I hear your faltering heart

thumping in the lifeless wood;
your fingers linger
like Orpheus looking back.

The Bell

At first, it comes at you from a distance, faintly:
a faded letter
about someone very old and far away
and only vaguely related.

You are urged to cry in public by your mother
and you do, respectfully,
but you don't really feel it.

Then it strikes closer to home.
There's a phone call about an older friend,
or a favorite first cousin or your grandma.
You see your mother weeping convulsively in the kitchen
and you measure the vociferous pain of her loss
against the silence of your own deeper hurt.

Then there's that dreaded telegram:
You lose a close friend or a parent.
Or worse still, a child or a spouse,
a beloved brother or sister.

They simply step off the life train one day
at an unannounced stop
in the middle of nowhere:
"Cancer!" "Heart attack!"
And they're gone forever.

Life is a journey among strangers;
all with the same destination.
Each stop may be a final
parting–no time to say "I'm sorry," No chance to say "goodbye."
Each new meeting spawns a farewell.
Each hello implies a goodbye.

Our lives are filled with many dyings.
Each one bares away a portion of ourselves;
each one, a rehearsal of our own deaths.

We watch some go lingeringly.
Pain sets the iron boundary of their being
as they unremember the events of their lives,
like a yo-yo gliding back up the string.

We plan a sudden, painless death for ourselves,
but not today, not just now.
We are still bewitched by life's enchantment.

Then the Grand Conductor taps you gently
on the shoulder one day,
saying, "Hey! Buddy, check your pass?"
And you know that the faint light at the end of the tunnel
signals your own stop.

The whistle blows hoarsely.
You gather up your meager belongings

and shuffle off to eternity:
wind in your face,
a stammer in your gait,
saying, "What a ticket! What a ride!"

Ascension

I stand in this empty parking lot,
listening for the cries, the laughter,
40 years gone,
blown into the past by these desert winds.

Where is the magic of those transient nights:
the bar fights, the liaisons,
the dreams sent up like prayers to the rafters?

Vanished, now, beneath this pavement
into the maw of space/time:
the bar, the piano, the jukebox.

The wind blows a piece of trash across the spot
where the bar stools spun;
a bird drops a speck where the pool table stood.

Where is the music from the jukebox now:
The words of the poets who ranted and strutted here?
The dancing, the actions,
all that energy buried beneath this asphalt.

This parking lot,
the roof of another world dissolved into memory.
Life is like a building with a one-way elevator going up.
Each floor, a unique chapter in our lives,

a different place in time,
sealed forever by history.

We climb through the stories of our lives
like Sherpas on the way to the summit.
Born in the basement among strangers,
we die on the roof alone,
Like birds.

New Year's Eve 1994

Home alone, trying to hold on;
getting dressed to go downtown to play a solo piano gig
for the early diners at the Cafe Centrale.

I search my closet for just the right jacket and tie
to match the dark bronze slacks I intend to wear,
and I wonder vaguely which ones she would have chosen.

Then I walk to the bathroom to shave,
and it hits me like a wave of nausea.
The first year of her demise is ending.
There's something inexorable about its closing.
An aloneness, a sense of rootlessness,
that I've never felt before settles over me.
She is gone.

I grab the sink with both hands
and the volcanic flow erupts once more.
I weep wantonly:
for myself, not for show,
but privately, to heal the injury to my soul.

It is 5:30 on New Year's Eve of her death year.
The year is closing and there's nothing to be done:
Nothing I can do to stop it, to hold it back.

The turning of the year finalizes her passing,
stamps it into history,
puts it beyond my reach, somehow.
I want to freeze the hands of time,
block them from swinging toward midnight.

Then I realize it is this pain of loss,
this grieving that makes us human.
And I ask myself if it's worth it,
if there's a lesson in the pain.

Losing my mom was not supposed to hurt like this.
She was eighty-three and scarcely recognized me
at the end.
Sitting in her wheelchair,
naked beneath a flannel robe,
she peed quietly into her Depend under garments as we
spoke.

It wasn't intended to end that way.
I wanted her to live in a big white house on the hill
with liveried servants to answer her beck and call.
There would be a limousine to whisk her off to
her appointments.

She would fade away gracefully with me by her side
to postpone her leaving,
to hold her hand when the end came.

Instead, she died quietly in a rented wheelchair
in a distant city among strangers,
with no one to comfort her.

I stand in my doorway,
feeling the chill wind rush up the corrugated metal stairs,
and across the porch toward me,
jostling the dry, dead leaves of another spent autumn.
I sense that she is no longer there
to nurse me through the failures,
no longer there to celebrate the victories.
And I doubt that I'll ever get over this,
that it even makes sense to try.

Then, suddenly, the mantle of her strength,
a strength tempered by the slings and arrows of
outrageous fortune,
flows into me:
My spiritual inheritance.

So I blow my nose,
put on my best jacket,
and call for a taxi.

Time And Place

TIME AND PLACE NOURISH OUR MEMORIES AND DETERMINE WHAT POSSIBILITIES ARE AVAILABLE.

Across a Bridge From the Sixties

J. Town! Juazoo! Juaritos! Call it what you would.
Juarez, Mexico, in those tumultuous times
was like an aging, overweight prostitute on the make:
lustful, eager to bargain, determined to give satisfaction.

And we abused her wantonly:
buying up her magic, her music, her bargains with our
Gringo dollars.
With her sideshows and aphrodisiacs, we vaccinated
ourselves against the lunacy of the times: of Nixon, of
George Wallace, of the war in Vietnam.

Juarez was cheap booze and five-dollar whores
and shop owners hawking their black velvet paintings
and silver and chess sets made of onyx saying,
"Come in! Take a look. Wanna see my junk?"

The odors of refried beans and charcoal barbecue and
diesel fumes
and the distant smoke of burning tires
blended into an elixir that worked on us like
Spanish fly.
But though you scoffed at the gaudiness
and ridiculed her blatant harlotry,
sooner or later, Juarez always had her way with you.

Sooner or later–at a bullfight or a strip show or an all-night mariachi bar,
she bled her soul into yours a little
and filled you with her madness.

For me, perhaps it happened the night Kenny Peterson and I were crossing the bridge to America at four a.m. We parked his dusty old van at the apex of the bridge, where the U.S. and Mexico collide, and jumped out.
The safety ropes of both flags clinked in unison on the cold steel poles in a brisk wind.
>There was going to be a urination ceremony.
>We were just going to zip down and let fly at the cosmos, in order that we might be able to say, "somewhere ages and ages hence," that leaning together, we pissed drunkenly into the Rio Grande one fine October dawn, mingling our streams with the fluids of conquistadores and Indian chiefs and U.S. cavalry horses and smugglers.

Until old Kenny said,
"Hey! Hey, Man, I think we'd better get the hell out of here before we get arrested, before they pronounce us guilty by osmosis."

And the spell was broken.
And we were on our way back to the Sixties in America with Bob Dylan and cheap grass and homemade hallucinogens, on our way back to a revolution we thought was just around the corner.

But most certainly Juarez cast her spell on me the night I was drinking at Don Felix, then the White Lake, then at Las Fantasmas with Alfredo.
At six-five and 250 pounds, we called him "the world's biggest Mexican."
We feasted on barbecued cabrito and pollo al pastor at La Palenque where they roasted whole chickens on spits in the windows.
Then we stopped at Las Dunas for some ten-cent tequilas to bolster our highs against the coming dawn.

Leaving there at four a.m. we stopped to buy cigarettes from a street urchin with a grocery sack full of American brands for twenty-five cents.
As I ripped open my new pack and lit up, Alfredo was haggling with the kid over a blackbird.
The boy had it tied to a string around his wrist like a falconer.
The bird was a special friend to him, his street buddy! the kid said,
But Alfredo wanted the bird and he knew just the move to make to get it.

"Look," he told the kid, (and he must have been peering intently into the bird's eyes when he said it), "this bird is very, very sick. I am a professor at the University of El Paso and I know these things."

The boy grew very quiet.

"Let the bird go with me," Alfredo said, "and I'll take him to the best doctors in the United States. Otherwise, he'll be dead within a week."

"Is it true, Señor?" the boy asked me sadly.

"The professor knows a great deal about birds," I said, clasping Alfredo's arm to emphasize my point.

The kid paused to sell some cigarettes to another customer. Then, reluctantly, after giving his friend a little talking-to in Spanish, he slipped the bird into a skinny paper bag and handed him over for fifty cents.

And with a bird in a bag we swung down the street and around the corner to Tommy's Rendezvous, so "the world's biggest Mexican" could play chess with the old men at the back tables.

Between moves, he punched tiny holes in the paper bag with a ball-point pen so the bird could breathe. And we discussed how to smuggle him across the border.

"If that son of a bitch makes so much as one squawk," Alfredo said,
"I'll just have to shoot the border guard and drive on."

When it was Alfredo's move on the chess board, I went up to the front and had a few Cubas with Jaime, the organ player; then I sat in with him on the piano and listened to the place fill up with after-hours Anglos from El Paso.

Later, after Alfredo had won two and lost one, we headed for our last stop. The New Mint Bar was the very last place to get a drink before you hit the immigration check point on the American side.

It was a hot, dirty little joint packed with West German soldiers and rowdy recruits from Fort Bliss who reeked of whores' sweat and Tecate Margaritas.

They were on their way back to the Sixties in West Germany or Chicago or Vietnam.

So we finished our drinks and stepped out into the cool, dry morning and sailed over the bridge toward America with a contraband blackbird, a bird he set free one week later, beneath the front seat of Alfredo's truck.

And we were on our way back to the Sixties of being university professors and bar owners and womanizers and poets. We wrote poems and sang folk songs and marched in demonstrations against war and racial prejudice, trying not to let the panic of being almost thirty show through. I was writing poetry and sitting in on jam sessions at the Alley Cat and the Whoo's Club and Casa Loma out on Alameda. Learning to play the blues. I was working one of those seams in my life, trying to stitch the threads of a patchwork past to the ragged edge of an uncertain future.

Published in One Eye Eight Magazine, 1994

Down at Jonah's

Down at Jonah's,
 they play cool jazz on Sundays.
Clutching handfuls of ivory, wood and steel,
 they all sit there,
reaching back for something real–
something lost in the echoes of forgotten caves,
 when men first strung stumbling syllables into speech.

Down at Jonah's,
 When old Flash Jones blows tenor sax,
his tongue attacks each note
 like a doorman checking IDs, saying,
"Man, is you blue enough to get into this jam?"

Down at Jonah's,
 if you could listen long enough and deep enough,
There's a song of weeping you should hear:
 it chronicles the fury of the need
to shape a mouth,
 to blow a reed,
to heed the body's burning.

Down at Jonah's, down and down,
 Hammered through whiskey-soaked notes of the blues,
they celebrate the ecstasy of despair.

El Paso Outback

In the coyote distance before me,
beyond the mesquite and creosote bush,
way out there on the edge of my hearing
where the solitude of this world of practiced certainty
collides with the ceaseless rush of the freeway;
the constant drone of semis sets an iron boundary.

Overhead, the wispy ripple of a jet's contrail
seems strangely out of place.

In the foreground, the two of them play at agates in the
fading sunlight:
choosing shooters, scratching concentric circles into the
vagrant dust.
Like schoolboys with boundless futures,
they bowl their crystal spheres across rabbit tracks and
beetle trails,
etching their identities into this land's long memory
of wagon trains and mountain lions' paths and dinosaurs
and sea beasts.

As if this ritual contest between these two savages
could alter the course of history somehow.
As if the outcome of this game
could derail the cosmos if it doesn't come out right.

The sun pauses for a moment
to give life a chance to catch its breath,
to measure its reserves against the coming of another day,
then cascades over the mountaintop like molten lava,
sucking the hot darkness behind it like a shroud.

These two broken-hearted dreamers
chase errant marbles into the gathering shadows.
While into the silence of a desert sundown,
night creatures move cautiously out upon the sands.

And we, much older and wiser than schoolboys now,
scavenge for wood like Neanderthals:
to set a fire,
to warm our backs,
against the sudden chill of evening.

Desert Nocturne

The night slips in,
like a thief on the prowl,
looking for someone or something to claim for her own.

She snatches the heat from the rock walls,
then squats on the mountaintop,
spilling the chill darkness from beneath her mantle
all over the land and waits.
Until the sun shuffles in from the desert
to chase her away at dawn.

La Quinta: Room 227

I have grown used to the strangeness of these rooms.
They are familiar to me now:
the ice bucket, the TV remote,
the soaps–a small one for the hands, the larger one for bathing.
And the shampoo.
All tucked into a little wicker basket with a fresh washcloth.

And I ask myself,
why this couldn't have happened twenty years ago
in my randy youth,
when all I longed for
was a free room and a willing woman.

There ought to be hosts of virgins
to stain these glorious sheets
with the blood of innocence,
to celebrate my conquest of the corporate moguls.

Instead, I fantasize about the phone numbers
in my wallet that could lead to something;
then I lie down in darkness, alone.
The familiar anonymity is comforting;
this is home to me now.

The history of the room possesses me,
hammers its sad truth into the core of my consciousness,
and I cannot sleep.

They are with me:
the souls of those travelers who have come and gone
from here.
The aura of this room,
brewed from the timbre of their lives.

The ghosts of those who grieved here:
those couples who pledged to give it one more go.
Murderers, suicides–those forlorn wanderers
who stopped here for the night to lick their wounds:
Truck drivers, salesmen, conventioneers, serial killers.

The flocks of nights gone by:
wedding nights, liaison nights.
The lifeless husks of vagabond nights,
penned to the pages of time
like butterflies in a collector's album.
Nights when you laid your body down
on a wide, cool bed,
praying for God to take your soul by morning.

But they are gone now–those strangers,
their emotions vaporized,
like images wiped clean from the chalk board for the
next class.

It is that ritual of perpetual order
that blanches clean the imprint of history,
that annihilates time,
and dissolves the emblems of remembrance.
Crumpled sheets, hanging towels,
the empty bottles–they're all gone.

When I come in from work,
there's no trace of yesterday.
Only the eternal present
that murders the past every second.
Everything in its place again,
and I'm left to reckon with
these specious memories.

My Sister's Clocks

Austin, Gwen's house, Friday afternoon.
I sit at her bar alone,
surrounded by the ghosts of her past lives.

The relics of wrecked relationships litter the walls:
Leda and the Swan painted by Ernesto,
the Budweiser beer sign from Kenny Nelson,
the Dallas Cowboy banner from who knows who.

They came and went like patrons of a penny arcade.
She offered them the poison and the antidote.

Then the chiming clock in the bedroom bongs 11,
causing the phone to ring.
Certain that it's the same wrong number for the fourth time today,
I pick it up and answer, "auto zone."

"Would you happen to have a tail pipe for a 1994 Isuzu Trooper?"
The man's voice was low, ragged and metallic.
"Tail pipe, Isuzu, ninety-four;
let me check that out for you."

I lay the cordless phone down in my chair
and start for the bathroom.

Harriet the overweight Lhasa Apso snores in the corner
as I pass,
and I'm there.
"Stand close, piss fast, zip up and haul ass," Jim always
said.

I pick up a long roach near the edge of the basin,
strike a match and toke up.

Moments later,
back in the living room,
I remember the phone lying there in the lazy boy
like a dead fish.

I pick it up and sit down.
"Yep, we sure do. Got it right here in my hand.
Seventy-five ninety-five.
Name's jack."

Meanwhile back at Gwen's graveyard of dreams,
brimming over with skeletons,
the cuckoo clock clucks eleven,
while the chiming one strikes twelve noon.

And for the first time in my life,
I realize that what time it is
depends upon where you are,
how long you've been there,
and how much of it you have left.

Desert Rain

Wrung from the dry spring sky with pain,
like tears from a Barbie Doll's eyes it came,
trickling silkily down cloudy thighs,
toward earth's thirsting.

The scent of morning sunshine on damp straw
seeped through the sun-scorched air,
like the wine of virgins' First Communion,
spilled in the parched crevices,
ending the drought of innocence.

And all came forth into the dusty streets,
to witness the miracle of a bleeding sky.

Homecoming

We sacked the pleasure domes,
rutted with harems of concubines,
quaffed the forbidden wine of heathen kings,
then purloined their fortunes,
and squandered them foolishly.

I, like the others,
scattered my talents
like sprouted seed upon fallow ground.

After all the aimless wanderings
through foreign lands,
crossing ghostly bridges in darkness,
among tribes of sybarites,
I come home.
My ears ring with the sound of a distant fanfare.

I stand here,
like a stranger before these crannied walls:
my senses blunted;
my appetites in ruin.

With tattered flags flying,
I return, profligate,
jaded by revelry and spring wines.

Sleek unfamiliar hounds loiter at the gates,
and my nostrils burn
from the oak-scented smoke of the fatted calf.

The Wall

Panel 39 E. line 12 reads,
"Jerry Lee Roe."
I trace the letters in his name with my fingertips J e r r y,
inscribed in the shiny black granite,
quarried in Bangalore, shaped and polished in Vermont.

The memories beyond his name
flow through my fingers and into my heart.

Eons ago and miles from here,
we were young once:
struggled through adolescence together.
Sweet bird of youth shot down in the jungle of Vietnam.

Now this name, chiseled in stone,
the only connection I have to those remembrances:
our youth together in Austin, TX and a 1940 Ford coupe
named Fat Mouse.

At the end of his name is a plus sign.
"A diamond means dead.
The plus means MIA," said the lady at the tourist center.
But my friends said he died in Vietnam.

I fantasize Jerry living incognito,
in some small Vietnamese village,
grandfather to a tribe of Amerasian progeny.

Then I turn to follow the wall past all those names:
58,372,
names enough to fill a book;
each name a life, a soul departed,
souls enough to populate a small town.

The wall declines slowly to where it disappears
into the Earth,
like Jerry.

Jerry who went to war in Vietnam;
I who went to war in America.
What does it mean,
this name embossed in granite?

Something there is too casual,
too nonchalant about tossing his name up on a wall.
The presence of all those other names
diminishes the importance of each somehow.
This is America's wailing wall.
"Something there is that..."

Waiting Room

Women seated around the room talking smack.
Rachael Ray cooking up an Italian dish on TV.
A young man on the left suddenly answers a call on his
cell about something serious.
While I wait for the doctor to pronounce a verdict,
like an executioner.

It's this pain in my stomach.
Is it an ulcer? Or is it my pancreas:
the first symptom of pancreatic cancer?

The woman in front of me keeps clearing her
throat violently
like she's trying to get rid of a lump stuck in there.

Then there are commercials and Rachael returns,
discussing the filling for some pastry she's cooking up.

A lady comes to the door announcing names,
"Dominick Wilson, Mrs.Gonzalez."

The room is thinning out now.
Some patients leave smiling,
the thrill of relief visible in their faces.

Others shuffle toward the door,
shoulders slumped, heads slightly bowed,
bearing the secret of their doom deep within them.

I caress the smooth, hard wood of the arms of my chair.
They are so durable, so timeless,
as if they could last forever.
While inside my body, things are breaking down:
Molecules misfiring, bad genes kicking in,
evil viruses gathering for an assault on my kidneys,
my liver.

Now on the TV,
Ellen DeGeneres chatters about something
entirely irrelevant.
Meanwhile, I can feel my immune defenses buckling
under attack from those free radicals stalking through
my veins.
And I remember when free and radical was a good thing.
In the Sixties most of us longed desperately to be free
and radical.

The lady calls another patient, "Mr. Johnson."
And I stroke the wooden arms of the chair again.
They are so palpable, so real, so permanent.
No free radicals lurking in their grain,

And I speculate about my own sentence:
the blood I left at the lab last week,
the coded secrets it might reveal to the doctor.

And I realize that I've spent my life in a waiting room:
waiting for something to go wrong.
Looking for a signal that the end is coming:
a lump, a bloody discharge, a persistent pain.

Death comes in so many different forms,
like the flavors of ice cream at Baskin-Robbins.

What life comes down to is a problem in arithmetic:
the sum of your cholesterol plus the
hypertension numbers,
minus the hemoglobin count divided by the
glucose level,
over the algorithm of the arteriole sclerosis
times the coefficient of the PSA number equals…
If the numbers add up wrong, you're dead.

Now Ellen DeGeneres is cracking jokes,
while my body is locked in an epic struggle
for survival.
I weigh my options.
Should I just skip out of here
without seeing the doctor?
Without hearing about the telltale evidence

from those specimens left at the lab:
the blood, the urine, the fecal matter.
But what if there's something I need to know–
An indication, a prognosis.

Just then the door squeaks open again
and the lady calls,
"Mr. Weldon."

I rise resolutely,
my jacket slung over one shoulder,
following her stiffly down the narrow corridor,
where I will wait once again for the doctor
in the small, inner room with two straight-back chairs
and some dusty unrecognizable equipment in the corner.
Resigned to my inevitable fate,
I whisper to myself as I go,
dead man walking.

Epiphany

To those poets and prophets
who walked this deserted beach
in search of a vanished ocean,
but settled for an epiphany instead.

And now these scavengers for the truth,
ensconced in the bosom of the Earth,
would seek the solution of the equation:
land times sea divided by time.

The fossilized calligraphy
etched in the bones and stones,
blown dry by desert winds,
then baked then sanded then buried.

God speaking in tongues:
to the ghosts of those poets and prophets
roosting in the cacti and yucca plants.
Made restless by coyote howls,
they rummage through this land of bristling relics,
where God delivered a revelation,
decoded one syllable at a time
by those who would extrapolate a theory of origins.

This land of the last temptation:
where Jesus faced the devil down,

where the line between good and evil may be
clearly drawn
in the sands of this parched earth,
where spilled blood may be measured with accuracy
and victory made certain.

Homeless

Tryin' to shake these homeless blues,
walkin' these streets in a dead man's shoes.
All I got left is the shirt on my back
and 47 cents in my jeans.

There was a time I had the world in my hands,
born the son of a doctor man;
had a cabin in the mountains and a home on the range,
but it all soon slipped away.

And now I'm homeless, yall,
sleepin' outside too long.
Dispossessed,
ain't a thing I can call my own.

Last night I shared a bottle with a dying man,
ate half a pizza from a garbage can;
slept out in the alley in the freezin' cold,
then the rain began to fall.

Walked two blocks then went underground,
found a warm dry place beneath a bridge downtown.
If my momma could see me down like this,
she would surely pray.

Cause I'm homeless, yeah,
sleepin' outside too long.
Dispossessed,
ain't a thing I can call my own.

You see me comin' in yo Cadillac,
pass me by don't even look back.
You feel so smug with your diamond rings
and yo alligator shoes.

Well lemme tell you a story it won't take long,
everything you have today could soon be gone.
You got ten thousand in yo bank account;
but you just a check away.

From bein' homeless, yeah,
sleepin' outside too long;
dispossessed,
ain't a thing I can call my own.

In the home of the brave and the land of the free
ain' nobody out there worried 'bout me

Cause I'm homeless, yeah,
Sleepin' outside too long.
Dispossessed,
ain't a thing I can call my own.

Hymn to Spring

Perched on a naked limb,
he warbles a full-throated hymn to life.
Even as the bow twists in a chill wind,
he kindles hope in the midst of despair,
with the passion of renewal in his heart.

As if his solitary song could awaken the seeds and tubers,
jolt them into fecundity,
breaking the frigid grip of winter in this barren land.

He prophesies the coming resurrection,
with a power that could summon Lazarus from the tomb.

With the fervor of a seer,
he heralds the redemption of spring.

Coming Into Autumn

Autumn evenings,
when the clack of leather heels on a hollow sidewalk
echoes down an empty street.
And there's a chill in the air.

Somewhere, across a darkening park,
beyond me, beyond time,
a mother cries, "Johnny! Oh, Johnny!"
And the air is strangely tinted
with the thrill of fresh beginnings,
though my blood thickens for winter.

Autumn evenings,
when friends draw close
in the lee of a canvas awning
near the Upstairs Theater Downtown.

Inside, we sip hot apple cider
from tall, glazed glasses,
while the stage is set for the third act.

Autumn evenings,
that can murder the heart with silence,
coming home alone after the losses
to the solitude of empty rooms.
You make up your mind to try something new,

to take a chance,
to pursue the road not taken.

But it's the fifth game of the World Series;
your money's on the underdog
and the leaves are dying.

Autumn evenings,
there's all that bother of Christmas coming.
The season's almost half over now
and the odds are lengthening.

It's the fourth quarter;
your team is six points down
to the odds-on favorite
and the clock is running.

But there's the scent of roses riding on the wind,
and there still is time.

Autumn again,
the days are shrinking.
The air is thick with the smoke of bonfires
and there's a presidential campaign under way.

Autumn,
and I carry the memories of what I used to get
for Christmas
home in a snug, brown paper bag.

But though the leaves have fallen
and the fans are home now,
tending their fires,
there still is time.

Time there is for long shots and last chances;
    time to kick 5 billion footballs across 5 billion parks;
time to ready the heart for one more run for the roses.

Though the sun languishes
and the stars are dying,
as we glide into the shadow of entropy
on the back of this vagabond Earth,
there is time;
there is time still.

Ireland

Ireland! Land of Ire.
fatherless motherland.
Plucked and plundered by those who would
steal her magic.
Home of slaves who would be kings:
who would rather be happy than rich,
who would rather dance than rule.

Ireland...
Broken castles
filled with unicorns and one-armed leprechauns.
Home of Mollie Malone and Henry Parnell and Bernard Shaw, too.
Tongues that speak with drunken eloquence.
Stolen hearts that smile through tear-stained eyes.

Oh Danny Boy,
Like a motherless son,
slumming down the road,
in the company of a man-headed lion.
Slouching ever so slowly,
slouching toward...

A Farewell to El Paso

On her way out of town that windy afternoon in April, she dropped me off in the alley behind the Backdoor Lounge, like the old days, when I had been one of the owners. I kissed each of the children, Michelle last in her jeans and tattered shirt, and stepped out of the rear door on the driver's side.

With my hand on top of the car, I leaned in through her window to imbibe the aura of her presence, possibly for the last time. And for that one, hypnotic, still-life moment, as I turned to go into the bar, I wondered if there were anything I could say or do to stay the curtain.

I would sweep her into my arms, promising to give up Ramona and drinking, insisting that she mustn't go to Saint Louis or Chicago; that she couldn't just turn her back on the tremendous thing that had been between us.

But just then, as I bent down to kiss her, she raced the engine and said, with a smile in her voice, "I hope you write a lot of books," and drove away slowly, honking as she turned out of the alley and into the street.

No one had said goodbye; no one had said it was over. But somehow I knew that the magic that comes between two people–once in a lifetime, in a certain place, at a certain time–was spent.

As I swung open the dangling screen door of the Backdoor Lounge, it was the smell that hit me: that familiar amalgam of Pine-Sol and cigarette smoke and stale beer. I walked into the head and slammed the brick wall as hard as I could with my open hands and just stood there in front of the open trough, smoking a cigarette, pissing into my own tears.

Then I called Ramona on the pay phone in the hall. But she sounded cool and distant. And the farther my wife got out of town, the cooler and more distant Ramona grew. She was just too tired, or she had to work late on her second job. When we were together, it wasn't the same. The challenge had gone out of it for her.

A week later, her daughter, Margie, was found dead in a motel room by the maid –nude, alone, abandoned like the leftovers of some junkies' banquet. Ramona was heartbroken and publicly despondent, but not surprised. Margie had almost OD'ed at least three times before. Still, when the funeral was over, the party was over. And I was pretty sure that Ramona was through with me after that.

But how could she be so totally and completely in love with me one moment and then, I was her "teddy bear," her "life's love." So I pampered her, gave her gifts, but nothing changed.

Finally, when she refused to make love, I baited her with another woman. It worked. She was in bed with me the next night. And I was through with Ramona after that.

I was through with El Paso after that. There was nothing left but the echoes of memories through ghost town streets—streets I had walked with my wives, my children, my lovers–streets paved with broken dreams: full of strangers, now, who knew my reputation but not my name. And I began to feel old among so many strangers, lost among all those familiar streets.

So I dropped into the Backdoor one afternoon with my typewriter in one hand and my white cane in the other. Poncho helped me carry in my old tin foot locker and stow it beneath the table. A one-way ticket to Los Angeles nestled in my jacket pocket.

Poncho was taking me to the depot. Old Poncho. I had asked a lot of him over the years, demanded much from him as a friend and partner; and the son of a bitch had been there for me every time–through all our adventures: the bar, the gravity meter, the trip down the Amazon.

I sat down at the big table up front, and he and I and Paul dived into a big pitcher. I hadn't even bothered to find out if the train was running on time.

When Poncho brought another pitcher, though, I decided I'd better check. The voice on the phone said we had ten minutes to make the train.

I was juggling Paul's arm and my cane in one hand and my typewriter in the other as we raced across the tracks toward my passenger car. Paul and Poncho each had one end of my old army foot locker, the tin curling up on the edges. The porter helped them stow it and my other things in the luggage rack.

"You lost your cane tip there, Taylor," Poncho yelled as he and Paul scrambled off the slowly moving train.

Nobody had time to say goodbye. And yet, just as the violinist knows when he finishes the concerto where the really good part was, I knew that an important movement in the concerto of my life was ending.

I just stood there in the open vestibule of the train car, arms at my sides, paying no attention to the porter who was trying to show me where the fountain and the men's room were, letting the syncopated motion of the train control me. It was moving forward, impregnating a void inside of me with its priapic thrust into the future. I felt vaguely feminine and vulnerable. I wanted to weep or pray or jump through the open door of the gently swaying train.

But as it rattled out into the open desert west of Smelter Town, gathering speed, I mounted the narrow, crooked little stairway up to my seat, cautiously, wondering what there could be in California.

Autobio

I attended the Texas School for the Blind in Austin, Texas for ten years. Then, along with three other blind individuals, we became the first blind students to be mainstreamed into a public high school in Austin.

Subsequently, I earned a B.A. degree in English from the University of Texas at Austin in 1964. In 1966 I enrolled in graduate studies at U.T. El Paso, where I was hired as the first blind teaching assistant in the Department of English in 1967. That experience initiated a career as an English instructor that spanned 20 years at two different colleges and one university in Texas and California.

While teaching in the Seventies, I operated two successful businesses: Santay Publishing and the Backdoor Lounge. In partnership with Earl Norman (Poncho) Sloat, we opened the Backdoor Lounge in 1971. Our customers were a kind of eclectic mélange of bohemians, intellectuals, street dogs and artists. The walls were lined with original oils, water colors and photographs.

Against a wall near the front window that looked out onto Campbell Street sat a console piano with a steel pipe for one front leg. An acoustic, upright bass wobbled in the corner nearest the front window. We jammed spontaneously in the afternoons, evenings and sometimes even in the mornings. We hosted poetry readings, chess tournaments, and dart board competitions.

In 1973 I sold out to Poncho and his wife, Carmen, to seek a more creative challenge: college teaching and freelance writing. With assistance from Richard Santelli and Kathleen McGary, I compiled, edited, and published *Passing Through* — a major anthology of contemporary Southwest literature–in 1974. The book enjoyed a two-year adoption as a freshman reader by El Paso Community College where I was teaching at the time.

Realizing that a B.A. degree would not take me very far in the teaching profession, however, I left El Paso in 1978 to attend graduate school in California.

After earning a Master of Fine Arts degree in professional writing from the University of Southern California in 1981, I earned screen credits as a performer and contributing writer for "Beyond Blindness," a one-hour documentary narrated by Patty Duke and produced for National Public Television. That same year, 1981, I sold my first article to *Publishers Weekly*. I was a successful contestant on the *$25,000 Pyramid* in 1987. After teaching English courses at Los Angeles City College for six years, I returned to El Paso in 1991 to resume teaching at El Paso Community College.

I am presently at work on a book-length memoir, a portion of which was included in *Reading Lips and Other Ways to Overcome a Disability*, published in 2008. Most recently, my essay, "Wild Velvet," won the national competition for creative nonfiction essays sponsored by the National Federation of the Blind.

In addition to appearances on radio, television, and in films, I have performed public speaking engagements in Texas and California. I have worked as a professional musician (piano player-fiddler) in Austin, El Paso and Los Angeles.

I live in El Paso, Texas with my wife, Valora. I am the father of four children and grandfather of four magnificent grandchildren, all living in California.

My civic activities include service on the board of directors of the El Paso Lighthouse for the Blind, member of the *El Paso Times* Editorial Board, and member of the state board of directors of the American Council of the Blind of the state of Texas. I have served as President of the El Paso Chapter of the American Council of the Blind and vice chairman of the Citizens Advisory Committee to the Mass Transit Board of El Paso.

BIBLIOGRAPHY

The following is a chronological list of titles that have appeared in magazines and books and have won awards in national and international literary competitions under the name of W. Burns Taylor.

Just Breakfast: *Goodbye Dove*—1967

Merrily We Roll Along: *Goodbye Dove*–1969

Just Breakfast: *Passing Through: an anthology of contemporary southwest literature*—1974

To an Old Guitarist Aging: *Passing Through: an anthology of contemporary southwest literature*–1974

Editor, *Passing Through: an anthology of contemporary southwest literature*—1974

Shoestring Publisher: *Publishers Weekly*–1982

Night Run: *One Eye 8*–1994

Across a Bridge From the Sixties: *One Eye 8*–1994

The Right to Vote: *Texas Observer*–1996

Editor, *Before Winter:* Poetry Collection by Clare Aguirre–1996

Voting Rights for the Disabled: *The Braille Forum*—1997

Coming Into Autumn: Prize Winner in the Edwin Dickinson Memorial World-Wide Competition—1998

The Music of Sound: Prize Winner in the Edwin Dickinson World-Wide Memorial Competition–1998

The Way I See It: Editorial Column in *Frontier Voice*, El Paso, TX–1997

The Way I See It: Editorial Column in *Rio Views*, EL Paso, TX-1997/1998

Coming Into Autumn: *The Braille Forum*–2002

Raising Canes: *The Braille Forum*–2004

The First Star I See: *Reading Lips and Other Ways to Overcome a Disability*–2008

Nightscape: Prize Winner in the National Writing Competition sponsored by National Federation of the Blind–2009

El Paso Outback: *Boundless Anthology*, published by the Rio Grande International Poetry Festival–2010

Wild Velvet: Winner of the Creative Nonfiction Essay Prize, sponsored by the National Federation of the Blind–2011

Hands Like Eyes: published in *Ojo Del Lago*, Ajijic, Jalisco, Mexico–2012

Index of Poems

A Farewell to El Paso 126
Across a Bridge from the
    Sixties 94
After the Reading 23
America the Bountiful 60
Anonymous Caller 12
Ascension 87
At the Diamond
    Shamrock 18
Before We Say Goodbye 39
Breakfast Blues 5
Coming Into Autumn 122
Confession 34
Coronation 54
Dance of the Marionettes 21
Desert Nocturne 102
Desert Rain 108
Dilemma 68
Down at Jonah's 99
El Paso Outback 100
Epiphany 117
Etc. 33
Ghetto Christmas 62
Hands Like Eyes 3
Homecoming 109
Homeless 119

Hymn to Spring 121
In the Valley of the
    Shadow 8
Ireland 125
Jack Be Nimble 51
La Quinta: Room 227
    103
Let's Pretend 38
Miraculous Transformation
    35
My Sister's Clocks 106
New Year's Eve 89
Nightscape 6
Note Found on a Kitchen
    Table 36
Party's Over 14
Pianos 43
Preservation of
    Pestilence 56
Reflections 57
Sayonara 46
Scars 70
Seasons of My Heart 72
Sky Words 77
Street Scene 59
Surfside 32

The Bell 84
The Nineties: a View from
    California 24
The Poem I Might Have
    Written 30
The Wall 111
The Way to Armageddon 78
The Weather Report 50
The Wedding 55

To an Old Guitarist
    Aging 82
To Whom It May
    Concern 41
Travelers 75
Voices and Faces 16
Waiting Room 113
Who Let the Tiger In 66
Yesterdays 76

www.ingramcontent.com/pod-product-compliance
Lightning Source LLC
Chambersburg PA
CBHW050641160426
43194CB00010B/1756